Bridgeman   01628   486465

Spice girls. greatest hits

Wise Publications
London/New York/Sydney/Paris/Copenhagen/Madrid

exclusive distributors:
music sales limited
8-9 frith street,
london w1v 5tz, england.
music sales pty limited
120 rothschild avenue
rosebery, nsw 2018,
australia.

order no.am949290
isbn 0-7119-7352-0
this book © copyright 1999 by wise publications

music processed by paul ewers music design
book design by studio twenty

printed in great britain by
printwise (haverhill) limited, suffolk.

your guarantee of quality
as publishers, we strive to produce every book to the highest
commercial standards. the music has been freshly engraved and the
book has been carefully designed to minimise awkward page turns and
to make playing from it a real pleasure. particular care has been given to
specifying acid-free, neutral-sized paper made from pulps which have
not been elemental chlorine bleached. this pulp is from farmed
sustainable forests and was produced with special regard for the
environment. throughout, the printing and binding have been planned
to ensure a sturdy, attractive publication which should give years of
enjoyment. if your copy fails to meet our high standards, please inform
us and we will gladly replace it.

music sales' complete catalogue describes thousands of titles and is
available in full colour sections by subject, direct from music sales.
please state your areas of interest and send a
cheque/postal order for £1.50 for postage to:
music sales limited, newmarket road,
bury st. edmunds, suffolk ip33 3yb.

www.musicinprint.com

goodbye

words & music by richard stannard, matt rowe, melanie brown,
victoria aadams, emma bunton & melanie chisholm

-va - tion, you know there's a bet- ter way for you and me to be.

Look for the rain - bow in ev- 'ry storm. Fly like an an -

- gel, hea - ven sent to me.

Good-bye my friend.

(I

know you're gone, you said you're gone, but I can still feel you here.)

It's not the end

(You

D.%. al Coda

The times when we— would play a-bout,— the way we used— to— scream and shout,— we

ne - ver dreamt— you'd— go your own— sweet way.———

Coda

(No, no,—— no. no.——)

You know it's time— to say— good-bye,—

(No, no,—— no, no.——)

and don't for-get— you can re - ly,—

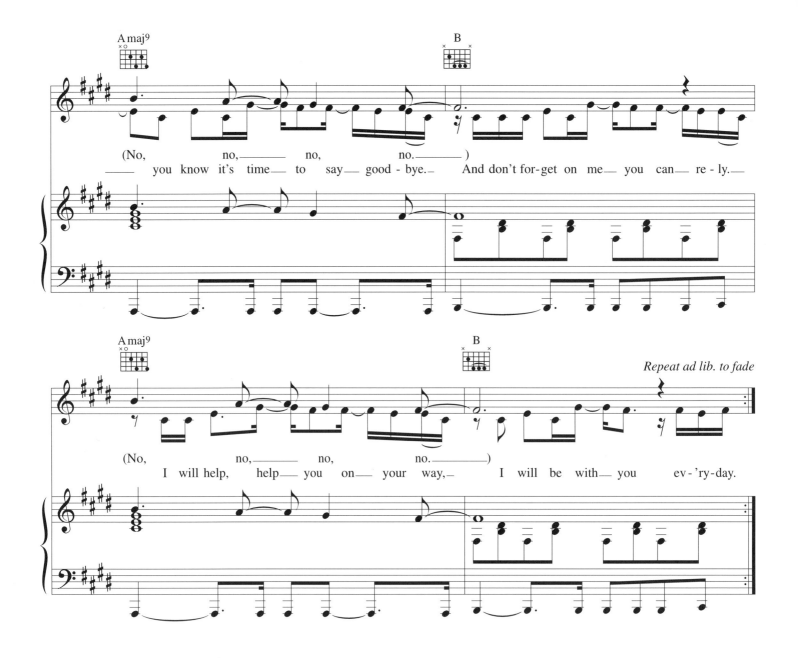

Verse 2:

Just a little girl, big imagination
Never letting no-one take it away
Went into the world, what a revelation
She found there's a better way for you and me to be.
Look for the rainbow in ev'ry storm
Find out for certain love's gonna be there for you
You'll always be someone's baby.

Goodbye my friend *etc.*

𝄋:
Look for the rainbow in ev'ry storm
Find out for certain love's gonna be there for you
You'll always be someone's baby.

mama

words & music by matthew rowbottom, richard stannard, melanie brown,
victoria aadams, geri halliwell, emma bunton & melanie chisholm

-n't be.   Eve - ry oth - er day I crossed_ the line,__ I did - n't

mean to be__ so bad,_____ I nev - er thought you would be - come_ the friend_ I nev-

- er had.   Back then__ I did - n't know why,__

why you were mis - un - der - stood.__   So now__ I

2. I

But now— I'm sure I know why,— why you were mis - un - der - stood.—

So now— I see through your eyes,—

all I can give—— you is love.—

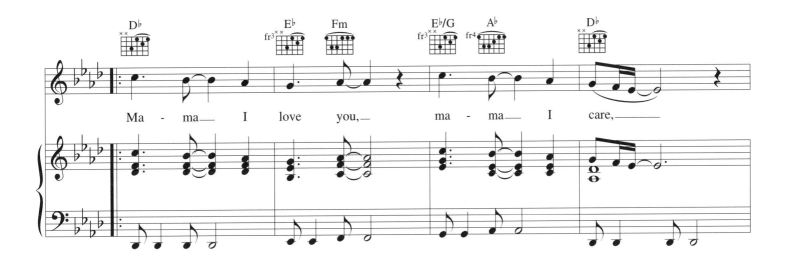

Repeat to fade

Verse 2:

I didn't want to hear it then but I'm not ashamed to say it now,
Every little thing you said and did was right for me.
I had a lot of time to think about, about the way I used to be,
Never had a sense of my responsibility.

Back then I didn't know why, why you were misunderstood.
So now I see through your eyes, all that you did was love.
Mama I love you, Mama I care,
Mama I love you, Mama my friend,
My friend.

do it

words & music by victoria aadams, emma bunton, melanie brown,
melanie chisholm, geri halliwell, paul wilson & andy watkins

1. It's just an-oth - er thing you got-ta keep your eye fixed on the road.—
(Verse 2 see block lyric)

Do what your Ma-ma said.— I will not be told.— Keep your mouth shut, keep your legs shut, get

back in your place.— Huh! Blame - less, shame - less dam - sel in dis - grace.———

Who———— cares— what they say— be-cause the rules——— are for break - ing. I'll tell ya

N.C.

You might do the wrong ____ thing for the right

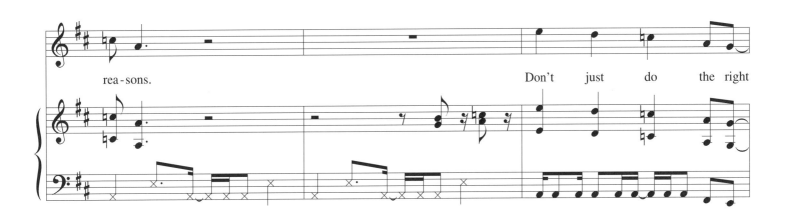

rea-sons. Don't just do the right

D.%. Repeat Chorus to fade

____ thing to be pleas-in'.

Verse 2:
Remember things like you should be seen and never heard
Give a little respect to me and it will be returned
Keep your head down, keep your nose clean, go back against the wall
Girl there's no way out for you, you are sure to fall.

Who cares what they do because it's yours for the taking
So, it's not for you anyway, make your own rules to live by.

Come on and do it. *etc.*

say you'll be there

words & music by eliot kennedy, jon b, melanie brown,
victoria aadams, geri halliwell, emma bunton & melanie chisholm.

that we had— this con-ver-sa-tion I de-ci - ded we should be friends,———— yeah.

But now we're go-ing round— in cir-cles tell me will this dé-jà vu nev-er end.—

Oh now you tell me that you've fall-en in love— well I nev-
(Verses 2 & 3 see block lyric)

- er ev - er thought that would be,———— yeah. This time you

Verse 2:

If you put two and two together you will see what our friendship is for,
If you can't work this equation then I guess I'll have to show you the door,
There is no need to say you love me it would be better left unsaid.

I'm giving you everything all that joy can bring this I swear,
And all that I want from you is a promise you will be there,
Yeah I want you.

Verse 3: (Instrumental)
Any fool can see they're falling, gotta make you understand.
To Coda

22

spice up your life

words & music by victoria aadams, emma bunton, melanie brown,
melanie chisholm, geri halliwell, richard stannard & matt rowe

When you're feel-ing___ sad___ and low, we___ will take you___
Yel-low men in___ Tim-buk-tu, col-our for both___

where you got-ta go.___ Smil-ing, danc-ing,___ ev-'ry-thing__ is free,___
me and___ you.___ Kung-fu fight-ing,___ danc-ing___ queen,-

all___ you need is___ po-si-ti-vi-ty.___ Col-ours of the world,___ ev-'ry
tri-bal space-man__ and all that's in - be-tween.__ (Spice up your life.)

boy and ev-'ry girl. Peo-ple of the world,
(Spice_ up your life.) (Spice up your life, ah!)

Slam it to the left (if you're hav-ing a good time), shake it to the right (if you know that you feel fine),

chi - cas to the front, uh_____ uh, go round._____

Slam it to the left (if you're hav-ing a good time), shake it to the right (if you know that you feel fine),

1.

To Coda ⊕

chi - cas to the front, uh, uh, hi ci_ ya_ hold tight.

stop

words & music by victoria aadams, emma bunton, melanie brown,
melanie chisholm, geri halliwell, paul wilson & andy watkins

1. You just walk in, I make you smile. It's cool but you_
(Verse 2 see block lyric)

don't ev-en know me. You take an inch, I run a mile.

Can't win, you're al - ways right be - hind me.

And we know that you could go and find some oth - er,

take or leave it or just don't ev - en both - er. Caught in a craze,

hu - man touch._____ Hey you, al - ways on the run. Got - ta

slow it down ba - by, got - ta have some fun._____ have some fun._____

Verse 2:
Do do do do
Do do do do
Do do do do, always be together.
Ba da ba ba
Ba da ba ba
Ba da ba, stay that way forever.

And we know that you could go and find some other
Take or leave it 'cos we've always got each other
You know who you are and yes you're gonna break down
You've crossed the line so you're gonna have to turn around.

Don't you know *etc.*

too much

words & music by victoria aadams, emma bunton, melanie brown,
melanie chisholm, geri halliwell, paul wilson & andy watkins

1. Love is blind as far as the eye can see, deep and mean-ing-less
(Verse 2 see block lyric)

G7
A
F aug
make me won - der. Too much of no - thing is just as tough, I
Dmaj7
1.
G7
2.
G7
need to know the way to feel to keep me sat - is - fied. keep me sat - is - fied.
Bm7
C♯m7
fr4
Gmaj9
What part of 'no' don't you un - der - stand? I want a man not a
F♯7(♯9)
fr3
A
F aug
Dmaj7
boy who thinks he can.

Verse 2:
Unwrap yourself from around my finger
Hold me too tight or left to linger
Something fine, built to last
Slipped up there, I guess we're running out of time too fast.

Yes, my dear you'll know he soothes me (moves me)
There's no complication, there's no explaination
It's just a groove in me.

Too much of something *etc.*

the lady is a vamp

words & music by victoria aadams, emma bunton, melanie brown,
melanie chisholm, geri halliwell, paul wilson & andy watkins

got class. Char-lie's An-gels, girls on top,— hand-bags, heels, their

pis-tols rock.— Ba-by love— are so— glam queen,— sing the blues— a love—

su - preme.— Six-ties Twig-gy set the pace,— way back then she

Tempo I

had the face. That's all in the past,— le-gends built to last.— But she's got some-thing new,—

39

41

2 become 1

words & music by matthew rowbottom, richard stannard, melanie brown,
victoria aadams, geri halliwell, emma bunton & melanie chisholm.

be for real_don't be _ a stran-ger. We can a-chieve_it, we can a-chieve_it._

_ Come a lit-tle bit clo-ser ba-by,_ get it on, get it on,_ 'cause to-night_

_ is the night _ when two be-come one._ I

need some love like I nev-er need-ed love be-fore,_ (wan-na make love to ya ba-by.) I

had a lit-tle love now I'm back for more, (wan-na make love to ya ba - by.)

Set your spi-rit free,— it's the on-ly way— to be.——

Oh,———— oh,————

Verse 2:
Silly games that you were playing, empty words we both were saying,
Let's work it out boy, let's work it out boy.
Any deal that we endeavour, boys and girls feel good together,
Take it or leave it, take it or leave it.
Are you as good as I remember baby, get it on, get it on,
'Cause tonight is the night when two become one.

I need some love like I never needed love before, (wanna make love to ya baby.)
I had a little love, now I'm back for more, (wanna make love to ya baby.)
Set your spirit free, it's the only way to be.

viva forever

words & music by victoria aadams, emma bunton, melanie brown,
melanie chisholm, geri halliwell, richard stannard & matt rowe

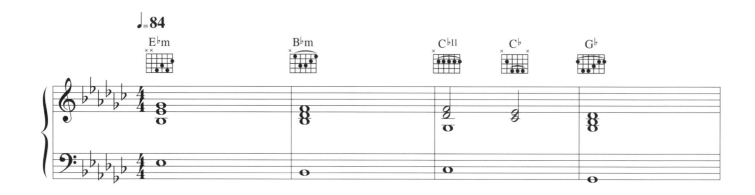

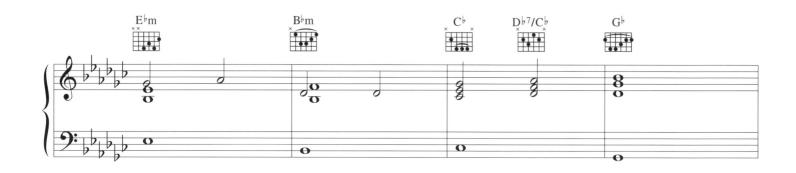

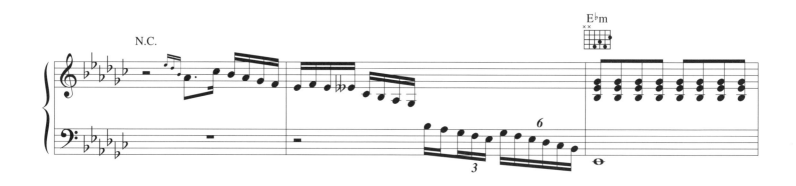

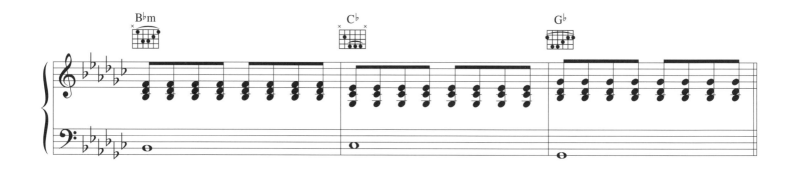

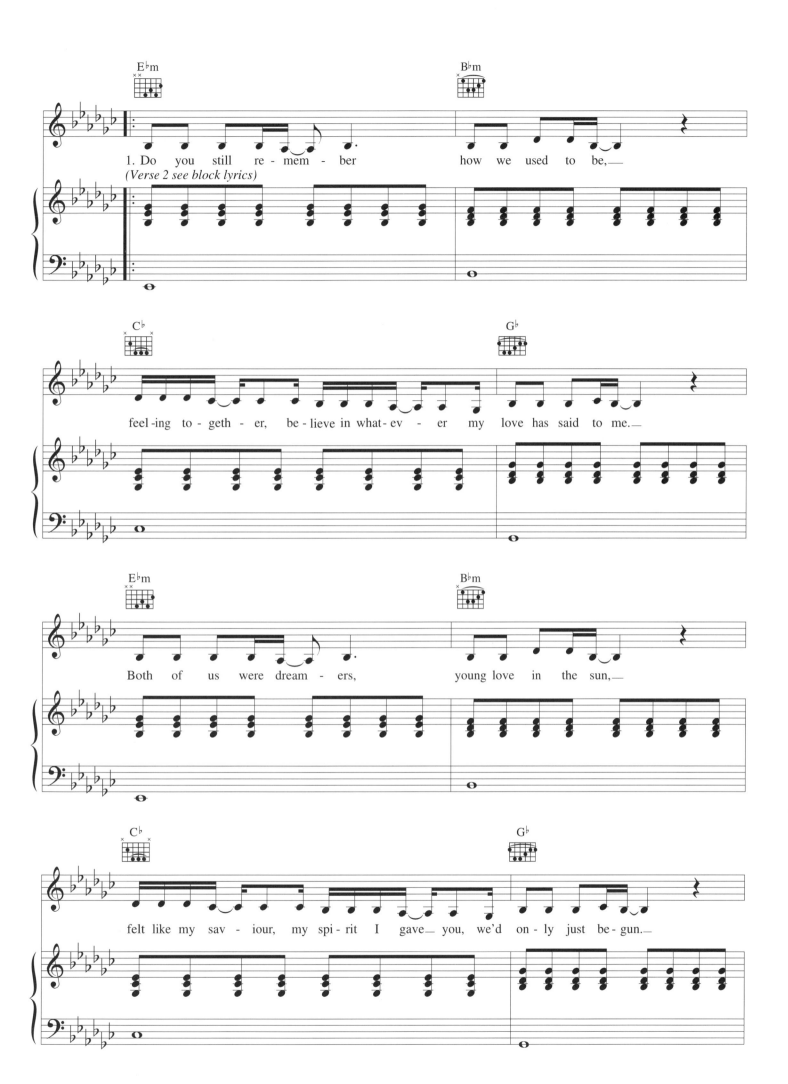

Back where I be-long— now, was it just a dream,-

feel-ings un-fold, they will nev-er be sold and the sec-ret's safe with me.—

Has - ta man - an - a,— al - ways — be

mine. Vi - va for-ev - er,— I'll be wait - ing,— ev - er-last-

Verse 2:
Yes, I still remember, every whispered word
The touch of your skin, giving life from within like a love-song that I'd heard
Slipping through my fingers like the sands of time
Promises made, every memory saved, has reflections in my mind.

Hasta manana *etc.*

who do you think you are?

words & music by paul wilson, andy watkins, melanie brown,
victoria aadams, geri halliwell, emma bunton & melanie chisholm.

1. The race is on to get out of the bot-tom, the top is high so your
(Verse 2 see block lyric)

roots are for-got-ten, giv-ing is good as long as you're get-ting, what's driv-ing you, it's am - bi - tion and bet-ting. I said who do you think you are? Do you think you are? I said who? Some kind of

show how good you are.

You have got to reach

on up, nev - er lose your soul.

You have got to reach on up, nev - er lose con - trol. I said

who_____ do you think you are?___ Do you think___ you are?___ I said

who?_____ Some kind of su-per-star, you___ have got___ to

swing it, shake it, move it, make it, who do you think you are?___

Play 7 times

Trust it, use it, prove it, groove it, show me how good you are.___

58

Swing it, shake it, move it, make it, who do you think you are?

Trust it, use it, prove it, groove it, show me how good you prove it!

Verse 2:
You're swelling out in the wrong direction,
You've got the bug, superstar you've been bitten,
Your trumpet's blowing for far too long,
Climbing the snake of the ladder, but you're wrong.

I said who do you think you are?
Some kind of superstar,
You have got to swing it, shake it, move it, make it, who do you think you are?
Trust it, use it, prove it, groove it, show me how good you are,
Swing it, shake it, move it, make it, who do you think you are?
Trust it, use it, prove it, groove it, show how good you are.

wannabe

words & music by matthew rowbottom, richard stannard, melanie brown,
victoria aadams, geri halliwell, emma bunton & melanie chisholm.

I wan-na, I wan-na, I wan-na, I wan-na real-ly real-ly real-ly wan-na zig - a - zig ha.

1. If you want my fu - ture, for-get my past. If you wan-na get with me,
(Verse 2 see block lyric)

bet-ter make it fast.— Now don't go wast-ing my pre-cious time,

get your act to - ge - ther, we could be just— fine.— I'll

Make it last for - ev - er, friend - ship nev - er ends.___

If you wan - na be my lov - er, you have got to give,

1, 3.   ***To Coda*** ✛

tak - ing is too ea - sy, but that's___ the way it is.___

2.

___ the way it is___

So here's the sto - ry from A to Z___ you wan - na

(2° vocal ad lib.)

63

Verse 2:
What do you think about that now you know how I feel
Say you can handle my love, are you for real?
I won't be hasty, I'll give you a try
If you really bug me then I'll say goodbye.